THE GLORY OF LIVING

A Play

by

REBECCA GILMAN

Dramatic Publishing
Woodstock, Illinois • England • Australia • New Zealand

IMPORTANT BILLING AND CREDIT REQUIREMENTS

All producers of the play *must* give credit to the author(s) of the play in all programs distributed in connection with performances of the play and in all instances in which the title of the play appears for purposes of advertising, publicizing or otherwise exploiting the play and/or a production. The name of the author(s) *must* also appear on a separate line, on which no other name appears, immediately following the title, and *must* appear in size of type not less than fifty percent the size of the title type. Biographical information on the author(s), if included in this book, may be used on all programs. *On all programs this notice must appear:*

"Produced by special arrangement with
THE DRAMATIC PUBLISHING COMPANY of Woodstock, Illinois"

THE GLORY OF LIVING

A Full-length Play
For 5 Men and 5 Women

CHARACTERS

LISA 15-18
CLINT. . . . . early 30s
JEANETTE / TRANSCRIBER . . . . late 30s
JIM / POLICEMAN #1 / DETECTIVE BURROWS . early 30s
CAROL. 19
HUGH / POLICEMAN #2 / GUARD mid-30s
GIRL. . . . . early teens
ANGIE . . . . early 20s
STEVE . . . . early 20s
CARL . . . . mid- to late 30s

THE PLACE: Various locations in Tennessee, Alabama
and Georgia.

THE TIME: The present.

*All persons and events depicted in this story are fictitious. Any
resemblance to real events or person is strictly coincidental.*

ACT ONE

SCENE 1

The interior of a small mobile home somewhere in Tennessee. About all that can be seen is a beat-up old sofa, a table of sorts and a TV. The rest of the trailer is blocked up by a big print sheet hanging from a rope strung from the walls. While the stage itself is minimally furnished, what is there suggests poverty and disregard. LISA, fifteen, enters, followed by CLINT NEEDHAM and JIM WATKINS, both in their early thirties. LISA is a tall girl, strong and slim with long, kind of ratty hair. She wears cutoffs and a T-shirt with some slogan on it. She is sullen and nervous.

JIM. God Almighty, girl. You wadn't kiddin' when you said that road was for shit.

LISA. I didn't say. My mama said. You want my mama.

JIM. Well, you ain't so bad. *(To CLINT.)* She ain't so bad.

CLINT. Shut up. You're insultin' the lady.

JIM. Shit. Where's your mama, gal?

LISA. She's asleep. *(She goes behind the curtain.)* Get up, Mama, there's a guy here.

JIM *(yells)*. Where's my Indian Princess? Huh?

CLINT. You're actin' like a pig.

JIM. Where's my gal that made me laugh?

LISA *(off)*. Come on, Mama. It's a guy.

JEANETTE *(off)*. What guy?

JIM. It's Whippin' Wizard, honey.

JEANETTE *(off, sleepily)*. Oh—hey! Hang on a minute, let me go pee.

LISA *(entering)*. She's goin' to clean up.

CLINT. How old are you girl?

LISA. Fifteen.

CLINT. You go to school?

LISA. Yeah.

CLINT. What grade you in?

LISA. Eighth.

CLINT. You make good grades?

LISA. Yeah.

CLINT. I went to school but I didn't make good grades. No sir. I was a troublemaker. Put a frog down a girl's dress once in third grade. Little tree frog. She liked to wet her pants. *(LISA laughs a little.)* Well, actually, she liked to wet her pants a lot.

(LISA laughs a little more.)

JIM. Y'all got anything to drink? Y'all got any Pepsi?

LISA. We got Fanta orange but it's my sister's.

JIM. Oh. *(Pause.)* You kind of a lanky girl, ain't ya? Isn't that what they'd call you, lanky?

LISA. I don't know.

JIM. What's your name?

LISA. Lisa.

JIM. Lisa. See, if you was to do like your mama and talk on the CB we could call you something like Lanky Sue, or Slim in the Saddle Sue.

LISA. My name's not Sue.

JIM. Yeah, but your mama's name ain't Indian Princess either, is it?

LISA. No.

CLINT. Tell her what "Whippin' Wizard" means.

JIM. Nah.

CLINT. Tell her.

JIM. Nah. She don't care.

CLINT. You ought to change that damn handle, man.

JIM. To what? Nightrider?

LISA. I like that.

CLINT. That one's mine.

(JEANETTE enters in a long T-shirt and shorts, looking made-up and pitiful.)

JEANETTE. Hey there.

JIM. Well hey there.

JEANETTE. Which one of you is the Wizard?

JIM. That's me. This is my friend Clint. I brung him just 'cause he wanted to go for a ride. He ain't got but to sit out here though.

JEANETTE *(to CLINT)*. I can do you too, if you want.

CLINT. No thanks. I'll just wait.

JEANETTE *(back to JIM)*. When did I talk to you?

JIM. Last night.

JEANETTE. Well I'm glad ya came by. You want something to drink? Lisa, go on and get them a beer.

JIM. Thanks.

(LISA exits.)

JEANETTE. That's my littlest girl. I got two others.

JIM. Where are they?

JEANETTE. Off somewhere. What you boys do?

JIM. Me and Clint work down in Chattanooga. At the U-Tote-Em.

JEANETTE. Y'all have trouble finding the place?

JIM. No ma'am. Them was good directions.

CLINT. Clear as crystal, I'd say. You got a gift of expression.

JIM. We saw the CB antenna right away when we was comin' by. Y'all need ta fix that road.

JEANETTE. The county's got ta fix that road, mister. I ain't fixin' nothin'. *(She looks at CLINT.)* You can talk to my girl while you're here but don't you go tryin' to mess with her.

CLINT. I was just—

JEANETTE. She went and hit a boy last month tried something with her. She's big for her age.

CLINT. Shoot, she's just a girl.

JEANETTE. Here, you come on back here with me, Wizard man.

JIM. My real name's Jim.

JEANETTE. It's good to know you, Jim.

(They go behind the sheet. From the movement it is obvious that the bed is only a few feet from the "living room" and that the sheet is the only divider. We hear LISA from behind the sheet, as well. What follows comes from behind the sheet.)

LISA. Here's your beer, mister.

JIM. Thanks.

LISA. You're welcome.

JEANETTE. Go on now.

LISA. Mama, can I watch TV?

JEANETTE. Go ahead.

LISA. Is that man still out there?

JEANETTE. He's okay, honey, he's nice. Ask him to
    watch TV with you.

LISA. Okay. *(She enters.)* Here's your beer, mister.

CLINT. You can call me Clint.

LISA. You wanna watch TV?

CLINT. Sure.

LISA. We only get two stations.

CLINT. That's okay.

LISA *(turning on the TV)*. When Mama talks on the CB
    though, we get three. Why is that?

CLINT. Something to do with the reception.

LISA. Yeah, I guess.

CLINT. You know how a TV works?

LISA. No. I kinda do I guess. I don't know.

CLINT. Here's how they do it, okay? They take the picture
    you're seein', and they bust it up into a kijillion pieces,
    and they send it out over the air waves. Then your an-
    tenna, it sorts out all the pieces, and puts 'em down inta
    your TV.

LISA. That is so stupid.

CLINT. Is not.

LISA. That ain't how it works at all.

CLINT. Tell me how then.

LISA. I don't know, but that ain't it.

CLINT. You're a smart girl, huh?

LISA. Yeah.

CLINT. Smart, all right.

LISA. Smarter than you, maybe.

CLINT. Oh yeah. *(He leans over and kisses her hard on the cheek.)*

LISA. Hey! Cut that shit out!

JEANETTE. What's going on out there, Lisa?

LISA *(thinks for a second, looking at CLINT, trying to decide whether she should tell on him)*. Nothing.

JEANETTE. Shut up then.

LISA. Okay.

(JEANETTE laughs and cries "Hey!" and the sheet shakes.)

CLINT. Your mama always do that sorta stuff with you right in the room?

LISA. It ain't the same room.

CLINT. It's the same room, darlin'.

LISA. She does it but I don't care.

JIM. Oh that's nice. *(Pause. CLINT and LISA stare at the TV.)* That is, that's nice. Come on an' take your panties off too, honey.

LISA. I really don't mind on account of it happens all the time. *(Pause.)* So I guess I'm kinda used to it.

CLINT. You ain't used to it and you ain't smart.

LISA. What's that mean?

CLINT. You ain't used to it. I can tell by how you got yourself all bunched up on the couch like. I study people, you know. I study body language. You ever been in prison?

LISA. No!

CLINT. See? Smart girl. Now in prison, there's guys that'll hate you for nothing at all. For being white or for bein' a nigger, it don't matter. They hate you is all. And them nigger boys is the worst, 'cause they stick together and you maybe do one of 'em wrong and then they're all tryin' ta kill ya. So you learn to read body language real good. 'Cause maybe this or that nigger don't care nothin' 'bout you, or maybe he's out for you. So while a nigger's comin' you're figurin' things up, whether his hands is just crossed like that, or whether he's got 'em set there to grab up a knife. You gotta figure all that out in sometimes just five seconds.

LISA. You ever get beat up?

CLINT. Nuh-uh, honey. Not me. I learned how ta read people and I became people's friend. I smiled all the time, like I do now, ya see? I smiled. You should try it too, smilin'. You might like it.

LISA. I smile plenty.

CLINT. So see, honey, I can see as how you're not comfortable with what your mama puts on.

LISA. So?

CLINT. So maybe you'd like to get the hell out of here.

LISA. I ain't going anywhere with you.

CLINT. Did I ask you to? No. That's where you're not so smart neither. For instance, a minute ago you didn't have no idea I was goin' to kiss you on the cheek, did you?

LISA. No, 'cause only a low-down fool would do that.

CLINT *(laughs)*. You got me pegged, gal! That's me. A low-down fool.

LISA. You think that's funny?

CLINT. I do. Maybe you ain't so dumb at all.

LISA. Maybe you don't know nothin' about it.

CLINT. That's a fact.

(Pause. As soon as they stop talking, they become aware of the sounds of lovemaking coming from behind the curtain.)

LISA *(shyly)*. How come you were in prison?

CLINT. Well, that's a silly story, but I stole some cars.

LISA. How many?

CLINT. Well, just one at a time. But I started around when I was fifteen or so.

LISA. Like me, huh?

JEANETTE. Ooh, baby, don't touch me there it tickles.

JIM. Okay then here! *(JEANETTE shrieks.)*

CLINT. She okay?

LISA. She's all right. She's a screamer.

CLINT. Oh. *(Pause.)* So anyway, I started stealing cars when I was about fifteen. Me and my friend Matt, we'd steal some little something and take it out by my farm and drive it about a hundred miles an hour down back roads. Then we'd dump it somewhere.

LISA. Cool.

CLINT. Yeah. We got busted off to juvenile homes a couple of times but that didn't stop us.

JIM *(off)*. Oh God, oh that's good.

CLINT. But then we got to our majority and they started a record, you know, repeat offender. Last time I got caught they put me up for fifteen months.

LISA. Man.

CLINT. Yeah, it really was a buncha nothin'. That judge, he said, "Son, if you behave yourself, you'll be out in six months." And I said, "Well then, Judge, I'll see ya in fifteen."

(LISA laughs. CLINT smiles at her and they look at each other for a few seconds. The sounds of her mother reaching orgasm are becoming painfully clear, as her moaning does indeed turn into a louder sort of screaming.)

JIM. Oh God yes, oh God yes, oh yes, oh, I'm comin'! I'm comin'! I'm comin'!

(The two seem to reach orgasm together and there is a moment's heavy panting and breathing. Pause.)

LISA. She fakes it.

CLINT. How do you know that?

LISA. She tole me.

CLINT. Where's your daddy?

LISA. He died.

JEANETTE *(off)*. Ow!

JIM *(off)*. Sorry.

LISA. He wrecked his motorcycle when I was ten.

CLINT. I think you're real special.

LISA. Special how?

CLINT. I kinda like the way you look.

LISA. I ain't nothin' to look at.

CLINT. Yes you are, gal. I ain't never seen anything as pretty as you. *(Beat.)* You like me?

LISA. I like you okay.

CLINT. You're a good listener. You don't just pretend. *(Beat.)* You wanna go out in my truck? Ride around?

LISA *(considers)*. Can we go down ta the quarry?

CLINT. You gotta show me where it is.

LISA. There's a junked up old car down there. There's like, just the seat, ya know. Just the old seat, an' some of the sides of the car, but there ain't no roof. You can sit in there.

CLINT. Sit in there and do what?

LISA. Lean back. Look up.

CLINT. You just show me where, sister.

LISA. Okay.

CLINT. Okay. Now you're so smart. Tell me what I'm going ta do.

LISA. I don't know.

CLINT. Tell me where I'm gonna kiss you.

LISA. On the mouth?

CLINT. See. Told you you was smart. *(He kisses her. Blackout.)*

SCENE 2

Lights up on the interior of a cheap motel room. The same furniture from before can be used in a different configuration. LISA and CLINT are lying in one of the beds, naked. They are arranged so that the heads of the beds are R or L, so that the audience cannot see behind the bed. CLINT is eating potato chips out of a plastic bag.

CLINT. We don't gotta go down there, honey. I just thought, that maybe once, you could see things the way I do and support me in tryin' to get somethin' good for us.

LISA. I always support you.

CLINT. You do not.

LISA. I do too. I been all over this damn state supportin' you.

CLINT. Who does the work around here?

LISA. Nobody.

CLINT. Who done it before?

LISA. I could work if you let me.

CLINT. Uh-uh, gal, you cannot. You got no diploma.

LISA. Neither do you.

CLINT. Uh-uh. They'll take you away from me again. I ain't sittin' in no goddamn jail again while you go out getting it with some goddamn nigger, gettin' it on day and night with some goddamn nigger.

LISA. Hardly.

CLINT. Don't talk like that to me.

LISA. Hardly gettin' it on with nobody.

CLINT. You said.

LISA. I said nothin'. Nothin' is what I said. Hell. I couldn't a got it on with nobody. I was big as a fuckin' house.

CLINT *(conceding)*. That's true.

LISA. And then my cooter was all ripped up to hell and sore. Hell it was sore. And they shaved off all my hair down there and man did it itch. Shit.

CLINT. Aw, honey. I can't believe I wasn't there for you, with you goin' through all that sufferin', and me beggin' them sons a bitches, sayin' "Please. You just gotta let me out, please. My wife is havin' a baby."

LISA *(quietly)*. Two babies.

CLINT. I didn't know that then. If I'd a known that I woulda asked twice as hard. "Please please, mister, you gotta let me go, I'm gonna be a daddy."

LISA *(laughs)*. I like the way you say that, "I'm gonna be a daddy!" It makes you sound like a little boy.

CLINT. And you're my little girl. *(He strokes her hair.)* You are all there is, Lisa girl.

LISA. Ha!

CLINT. It's true.

LISA. Ha ha!

CLINT. I don't care if you don't believe me, it's the God's truth.

LISA *(pause)*. Clint, I wanna see the twins.

CLINT. We'll go up to my mama's soon an' get 'em.

LISA. They're at my mama's.

CLINT. They ain't.

LISA. They are too.

CLINT. Girl, your mama's a whore. We did not leave them with your mama.

LISA. I thought we did.

CLINT. Girl, your mama is a drunk whore.

LISA. Yeah, so? *(They laugh.)*

CLINT. Aw, honey, I don't know if you can feel it, but pretty soon you and me is gonna be set. There ain't gonna be a single town that hadn't felt us comin' and goin'.

LISA. Where's your gun? I wanna see your gun.

CLINT. I don't wanna get up, honey.

LISA. I wanna see it.

CLINT. I don't wanna get up, honey. I'm all comfortable like I am now. Right here like I am now.

LISA. I wish you'd let me see it. I like it when you let me hold it.

CLINT. Hold somethin' else, gal, right under here. *(He lifts up the sheet.)*

LISA. Can you do it again?

CLINT. What's that s'posed ta mean? Huh? *(She doesn't answer him.)* Answer me, Lisa gal.

LISA. It don't mean nuthin'. It just means, I wanna do it again too. If you wanna. If you don't neither, that's okay. That's okay too.

CLINT. I tell you this once and you hear me good. Hear me good, girl. I can do it whenever I goddamn please. You hear that? I can do it whenever I goddamn please!

LISA. Okay. I'm sorry.

CLINT. You fuckin— *(He shoves her violently out of the bed, onto the floor.)*

LISA. Okay, okay, okay. *(She gets up. On her naked body we can see a host of bruises. She walks quietly over to the bathroom door and goes inside.)*

CLINT *(yelling after her).* Where're you goin'? You bitch. Go in there and wash me out. Go in there and wash me out of you. I know that's what you're doin'.

(He reaches over the side of the bed, upstage from the audience, and grabs something heavy and starts to pull. It is a slight GIRL, around fifteen years old. She is handcuffed to the headboard and she is wearing a T-shirt and panties. She seems to be unconscious but as he starts pulling on her she starts to moan.)

CLINT. Get up here! Come on, you little chit, get up here! *(He pulls her onto the bed with him, and then lies there for a second, recovering his breath from the effort.)* Jesus. *(Pause.)* You awake? *(She doesn't respond. He starts to prod her.)* Hey? Girl? You awake? *(He shakes her.)* Wake up! I wanna talk to you. You still sick? *(She groans.)* You look sick. *(Beat.)* You prob'ly never got

drunk before, huh? I bet you hadn't. We maybe
shoudn'ta made you drink all that. Lisa one time gave
one of the babies a drink. Made it sleep for hours. I said,
"That's good stuff." *(Pause.)* "We oughta bottle that
and sell it for cough medicine." *(Pause. He starts rub-
bing her stomach over her T-shirt.)* We done lotsa stuff.
Me and Lisa. Mostly me though. I robbed a Jitney Jun-
gle once. They got those in Alabama? They got 'em in
Florida. They're just like a Mini Mart, only better.
(Beat.) I was gonna rob some more, maybe. But I got
sent up for a while, for kiting checks. Well, for stealing
too. From the U-Tote-Em where I worked. Took shit all
the time. *(Beat. Fondly.)* Lisa useta come to work with
me. I'd lay her down on the floor of the cooler, on that
cold cement floor, and I'd do to her what nobody else is
done to her. I'd turn her legs up and go to it. She'd say
it hurt her back, on that cement floor. I'd say "Good.
It's suppose ta hurt. It's the best kinda hurt there is."
She didn't really mind it. *(Beat.)* Lisa likes you 'cause
you was in a juvenile home too. Wadn't you. *(He starts
to pay a little more attention to her.)* You're kinda
pretty. *(He starts to pull her T-shirt up. He stops half
way and starts to rub her stomach again.)* You sick,
huh? My mama useta rub my tummy like this when I
was feelin' sick. She'd give me a warm Coke and she'd
rub my tummy and hum, hum, hum. *(Pause, he tenderly
rubs her stomach, making small circles with his hand.
He hums tunelessly.)* 'Course I don't know no songs.
(He stops and looks at her.) Lisa knows this, and she
knows how I hate for her to say this out loud to me, but
I sometimes can't do it more'n one time a day, on account of how much I put out at a time, and my resources

can't build back up too fast. 'Cause of the output. *(He pulls her shirt back down. Pause. He looks at her. He calls.)* Lisa! Come on out here, gal. I ain't mad no more. *(Pause.)* Come out. I'm sorry I shoved on you. I ain't mad at you. Come out. *(The bathroom door opens a crack.)* Come on.

LISA. What for?

CLINT. Come on.

LISA. What for?

CLINT. You hear me, don't ya?

LISA. Okay. *(She comes out with a towel around her.)* How come you got her up on the bed?

CLINT. I ain't doin' nothin' with her.

LISA. What you want me for?

CLINT. Come on over here and see if you can wake her up.

LISA. She ain't hurtin' nobody.

CLINT. I know. Come on over here.

LISA. She's a little girl.

CLINT. Come on. *(LISA makes her way, haltingly, to the bed.)* Lay down here between us. *(She crawls between them.)* Let's all get under the covers, nice and family like.

LISA. You ought to unhook her, it'd be easier.

CLINT. Uh-uh. I don't think so. Now here. You lie there and see if you can't wake her up. I wanna watch you try.

LISA. How?

CLINT. Nice like. You rub on her and you kiss on her and you see if you can't wake her up.

LISA. I don't know how.

CLINT. Oh yes you do, baby. You know you do. Go on now. I wanna watch.

LISA. I don't know how.
CLINT. Oh yes you do. *(Blackout.)*

SCENE 3

The lights come up on the GIRL, still in the bed. She is awake now and sitting up, hugging her knees, with the sheet pulled up around her neck. LISA is getting dressed. She is rooting through a duffel bag, looking for some jeans.

LISA. I just, I just can't find anything in here. It's such a mess. Me and Clint, we ain't normally this messy, you know. We just, well, we been on the road for a while now and you know ... living in motels. *(She giggles nervously.)* You get useta the maids an all. *(She pulls out some jeans and smells them. To herself almost.)* These ain't too bad, I guess. Sometimes they get that cum smell on 'em ... I mean, you know.
GIRL. I know.
LISA. You do?
GIRL. Yeah.
LISA. You thirsty or something?
GIRL *(almost crying).* I really gotta go to the bathroom, please, I gotta go so bad.
LISA. Oh. Okay. I mean, oh. I don't know what to do.
GIRL. Please. I'm gonna go in my pants. I hurt so bad.
LISA *(starts looking around aimlessly).* Okay. Okay. Okay. I'll just, I'll just unlock these things and go with you. But you gotta promise not to run away.
GIRL. I promise, please.

LISA. Okay. I'm gonna unlock these things. I'm a mama, you know. I know how it gets bad and all. *(She unlocks her.)* Okay. You go in here, just go in an I'll close the door. You go on. *(The GIRL limps into the bathroom and closes the door.)* Just tell me when you're through. Okay?

GIRL *(off)*. Okay.

LISA *(putting on the jeans. Talking to fill the time)*. After this we gotta go somewhere. It ain't far but we gotta go. I'm gonna go get my kids first. They're up at my mama's. And then we're gonna go somewhere together. Just us. I got my own car. Me an' Clint, we gotta have separate cars, on account of how he sometimes has business he gotta take care of. *(Beat.)* We talk on the CB a lot though. In our cars. He'll call me up sometimes and pretend he don't know me an act like we're meetin' right there on the radio and arrangin' to go to some motel together. Just to keep things interestin' an' all. 'Count of how we been married so long. We been married two whole years. Come August. *(Beat.)* You doin' okay in there?

GIRL *(off)*. I guess.

LISA. You ready to come out?

GIRL *(opening the door)*. I guess.

LISA. You gonna flush?

GIRL. No.

LISA. You wipe?

GIRL. Yeah.

LISA. Okay. Sit down over there while I get ready.

GIRL. Okay.

LISA. Was you in that home long before you ran away?

GIRL. 'Bout four months.

LISA. You glad we give you a ride?

GIRL. I guess.

LISA. We coulda took you to the police.

GIRL. I'm glad you didn't do that. They caught me once before.

LISA. What'd they do to you?

GIRL. Took me home.

LISA. Is that why you was in that home? 'Cause you run away all the time?

GIRL. Nah. They put me in there for protection.

LISA. Oh. Somebody beat on you.

GIRL. No. It was this man my mama lived with. He useta come in the living room and make me lie on the couch, and he'd put his fingers in me.

LISA. I'll be glad when I turn eighteen. Then they cain't put me in them homes no more. They wouldn't a done it at all, 'cept Clint was in jail. And I was pregnant.

GIRL. I hate it there. The food sucks.

LISA. Yeah. They don't let you sleep late neither.

GIRL. Yeah. I hate that.

LISA. You look like a girl from TV. Like Joanie from *Happy Days*.

GIRL. Well, I wish that y'all would let me go.

LISA. How come?

GIRL. 'Cause I'm sick. He hurt somethin' in me.

LISA. He's real big. He made my gash bigger.

GIRL. He's mean.

LISA *(stops packing and stares at her)*. He is?

GIRL. Yeah. Anyway, can I go now?

LISA. No. I cain't let you. I'm sorry. But it's okay. I'm takin' you out of here. I'm gonna go get my kids and then I'm takin' you out of here.

GIRL. You gonna give me a ride?

LISA. Yeah. Where're your pants and stuff?

GIRL. Under the bed.

LISA. You get 'em and get dressed. You'll feel better. I promise.

GIRL. Okay. *(She crawls to the other side of the bed and disappears onto the floor.)*

LISA. I'm real sorry you're sick. None of this was my idea though. You gotta know that. Okay?

GIRL. Okay. *(Comes back up with some pink pants.)* I'm gonna put these back on.

LISA. Good girl. Just know it too, though.

GIRL. Know what?

LISA *(pauses)*. Nothin'. Never mind. I got just about everything.

GIRL. I can't find my shoes.

LISA. Clint took 'em.

GIRL. How come?

LISA. He's like that. But you don't worry. You won't be seein' him ever again.

GIRL *(almost smiles)*. Good.

LISA *(turns off the light)*. We gotta be real quiet. We ain't paid the bill. Now you just hold my hand and come on.

GIRL. Okay.

LISA. Be good now.

GIRL. Okay.

LISA. Be good. *(Blackout.)*

SCENE 4

*Lights up on a very similar motel room. The beds have a
different spread, but the atmosphere is the same. Dirty
and cheap. Again, of the two beds, only one has been
slept in and again, there are soda cans, candy wrappers,
etc., all around the place. CLINT sits on the bed, fully
dressed. CAROL, nineteen, sits next to him, eating from
a big bag of pretzels and drinking a Pepsi. LISA is yelling at CLINT.*

LISA. You can't tell me you don't like her! I drove around
all goddamn day tryin' to get one. You can't tell me you
don't like her! They ain't nothin' wrong with her. She's
nice.

CLINT. It ain't that I don't like her, honey. It's just that
she kinda gives me the creeps.

LISA. She's nice. Ask her somethin'. You'll see. *(To
CAROL, yelling.)* Tell him how nice you are!

CAROL. Y'all seem nice too.

LISA. See? See?

CLINT. I guess.

LISA. You ain't never satisfied with nothin' I do for you. I
could grow two heads and you'd still say I wadn't smart
enough. I could grow six legs.

CLINT *(laughs)*. You'd be a bug.

LISA. You ain't funny, not one bit funny. I been tryin' all
goddamn day. All goddamn day.

CLINT. Okay, honey. Okay. I'll talk to her. *(Turns to
CAROL.)* What's your name, honey?

CAROL. Carol.

CLINT. That's nice. This is Lisa an' I'm Clint.

CAROL. I know. How come y'all didn't want Steve comin' back with us.

CLINT. He didn't wanna come.

CAROL. How come y'all didn't give him a ride home? He doesn't like the woods. I don't think he wanted to stay in the woods.

LISA. Yes he did. He said so.

CLINT. Them pretzels good?

CAROL. Yeah. *(Pause.)* Can I have another Coke?

CLINT. Yeah. Sure. Here's fifty cents. You can go get it.

LISA. Clint!

CLINT. Honey, she ain't goin' nowhere.

LISA. Clint!

CLINT. Go on, Carol honey. *(He ushers her out the door.)* Lisa, calm down.

LISA. She's gonna call the fuckin' cops!

CLINT. No she ain't. Can't you see? She's simple.

LISA. Simple what?

CLINT. Simple. Touched. She's got somethin' wrong with her.

LISA. Retarded?

CLINT. Could be. There was a buncha kids in my school like that. They had a special class.

LISA. Oh.

CLINT. I useta pick on them kids somethin' awful till one day, my teacher, she sat me down and said, "Now, Clint, you're a lucky boy. You're smart and you got a way with people. Them kids, they's got no luck in this world at all, and then you go and heap misery on them, they don't deserve that." An' I seen right away how she was right. And after that, anybody went to pick on one them kids, I'd hit 'em so hard they'd shit theirselves.

LISA. Is that true?

CLINT. How come you question all I say?

LISA. It don't sound like you to stick up for somebody.

CLINT. Well I did and you better stop questionin' me 'cause it always sounds like you're mockin' me and I cain't abide that behavior at all.

LISA. Okay.

CLINT. You sorry?

LISA. I'm sorry, Clint.

(CAROL comes back in with another Pepsi.)

CAROL. Thanks, mister.

CLINT. You're welcome, honey. *(Pause. He looks at LISA while he says this.)* You wanna do somethin' else for me?

CAROL. What's that?

CLINT. You wanna take off your clothes?

CAROL. Oh. Y'all wanna do that?

CLINT. Yeah, honey. We wanna do that.

CAROL. Okay. *(She starts taking off her clothes.)*

LISA *(to CLINT)*. Shoot. Look at her. She's ugly.

CLINT. She's okay.

LISA. She din't even flinch when you asked her. She don't even care about her boyfriend. Hey. Hey, girl. What would your boyfriend say about this?

CAROL *(with her shirt over her head)*. I don't know. We never did this.

LISA. You a virgin?

CAROL. No. I done it lots with other guys. That's how I get rides home.

LISA. Oh. *(To CLINT.)* You look see she ain't got no bumps or nothin' on her. I don't want no twat rot.

CLINT. Where you learn that language? Your mama teach you ta talk like that? I swear.

LISA. I just don't want nothin' bad comin' of this. I feel nervous. I'm all on edge.

CLINT. Don't be. Go on now. Go on and go for a drive.

LISA *(crushed)*. Clint. I been in the car all day. I'm so tired. Please don't make me go. I can just lie on the other bed. I can just watch TV real quiet. Please, honey.

CLINT. Aw, sweetie. You know how you get. Now go on.

LISA. No. I promise I won't. I swear. Please. You know I'm different now. You know how different I can be. Please. Don't make me go.

CLINT. You don't wanna stay, honey. Now go. *(He gets up and starts pushing her slowly toward the door.)*

LISA. Please.

CLINT. No ma'am. *(He opens the door and pushes her out.)*

LISA *(near tears)*. Clint...

(CLINT pulls his arm back, as if to slap her. She steps back. He points his finger in her face.)

CLINT. You know. Don't mess with me. Here, take your purse. *(He shoves it at her and closes the door then turns to CAROL.)* See how she's devoted ta me? I swear I love that girl.

CAROL. She your daughter?

CLINT. Honey. That gal is my wife, thank you.

CAROL *(laughs)*. You're married.

CLINT *(looks at her)*. You wanna do this, really?

CAROL. Sure. Lemme drink some more Coke. Them pretzels make me thirsty.

CLINT. I bet. You know how to do it with your mouth?

CAROL. I know that.

CLINT. Well you're a real find. Lisa done good.

CAROL. Will y'all give me a ride back home?

CLINT. Of course we will, honey. Of course. *(Blackout.)*

SCENE 5

*Lights come up on the motel room, the next day. LISA is
alone. She is on the phone, waiting nervously.*

LISA. Hello? This the police station?... Um, no. I don't
guess it's an emergency. I just got some information. It's
about a girl. Up at Kentwood. State Park. Up there.
There's a, there's a um ... a missin' girl up there. She was
at the Harpstead Home. She ran away from there.
(Pause.) No ma'am. I don't know her name. But I seen
her body up there. *(Pause. Then quickly.)* No ma'am, I
cain't give you my name. You just, you just got to go up
there, if you go up there through the main park part, up
ta the parkin' lot, and then there's a lookout spot? Go up
there and look down in the canyon and you'll see where
they dumped her body. Down there. You'll see her if
you go up there and look. *(She hangs up quickly.)*
*(Pause. She looks around nervously. Then she crosses to
the TV and turns it on, gets on the bed and lies there,
her arms by her side, waiting. Blackout.)*

SCENE 6

The same motel room. Empty. The TV is on but that is the only light. Sounds of scuffling from outside, then LISA and CLINT enter. He is half-dragging her. They are both drunk.

CLINT. C'mon, honey. Walk on in. You just put one foot in front of the other. Just walk like when you was a baby. Just walk.

LISA. Clint?

CLINT. Yeah, darlin'?

LISA. I am so drunk. *(She begins to laugh.)*

CLINT. Lisa?

LISA. Yeah, darlin'?

CLINT. You are so drunk.

LISA. Shuddup!

CLINT. You are!

LISA. You are so mean!

CLINT. You are so drunk! *(They collapse on the bed, giggling. CLINT pulls LISA to him and holds her.)* Honey? Hey, honey?

LISA. Yeah?

CLINT. You wanna know somethin'?

LISA. What?

CLINT. You wanna know how much I love you?

LISA. How much?

CLINT. I love you so much it makes me sick sometimes.

LISA. That ain't nice.

CLINT. No, I mean it. Sick with worryin'. Sick with bein' jealous. I get crazy jealous over you.

LISA. I know.

CLINT. I see a guy lookin' at you, I wanna eat him alive.

LISA. Nobody looks at me no how.

CLINT. Oh, honey.

LISA. Uh-huh. I'm a ugly ol' hag. Ugly an' old as the hills.

CLINT. You're a goddamn baby. My goddamn baby girl. *(He strokes her hair.)* Honey?

LISA. Yeah.

CLINT. Promise you ain't never gonna leave me.

LISA *(beat)*. You know I ain't.

CLINT. Promise.

LISA. I promise.

CLINT. Me too. I promise you too. Don't you be scared a that.

LISA. I ain't.

CLINT. Sometimes, I look up at night, up at the ceilin' and I think as how all there is of me is right there. Right there floatin' between the bed an' the roof. I think I'm gonna wake up in the mornin' wishin' I hadn't. You ever feel that?

LISA. I don't think so.

CLINT. Look up at the ceilin' now. Tell me what it makes you think.

LISA. It makes me think the bed is spinnin'.

CLINT. Uh-oh. You got the spins.

LISA. Ugh.

CLINT. Close your eyes. *(He puts his hand over her eyes.)* Keep 'em closed.

LISA. I feel sick.

CLINT. Shhh. Shh. Keep 'em closed, honey.

LISA. Okay.

CLINT. You go to sleep now.

LISA. Okay.

CLINT. Go to sleep and I'll stay here. I'll stay here. I'll watch TV.

LISA *(quietly)*. Okay.

CLINT. Shhhh. *(He holds his hand over her eyes. Slow fadeout.)*

SCENE 7

Lights up on the same motel room. Next day. The TV is off but everything else is the same. LISA enters, throws down her purse on the bed.

LISA. Shit. *(She sits on the bed. Kicks at an empty can on the floor. She is like a pouty, disappointed child.)* They didn't even clean the room.

(Sound of a car door slamming. CLINT enters, in the same mood.)

LISA. They don't even clean the rooms around here. What's the deal?

CLINT. What'd you come back for?

LISA. I didn't wanna do it anymore.

CLINT. What about that one girl?

LISA. She wouldn't get in the car.

CLINT. Why not?

LISA. I don't know why not. She almost was, I think, but then she changed her mind.

CLINT. What'd you say to her?

LISA. I said, "You wanna go for a ride?" That's all.

CLINT. Shit.

LISA. I cain't help it.

CLINT. You can too.

LISA. No I cain't.

CLINT. We gotta get you cleaned up. I bet if you washed your hair they'd git in with you.

LISA. They don't care about my hair. They just know somethin' funny is gonna happen.

CLINT. What does that mean? Somethin' funny.

LISA. They just know. They're scared.

CLINT. 'Cause you're scared.

LISA. I don't act scared. I act normal.

CLINT. You don't know what normal is.

LISA. Don't be mad.

CLINT. I'm goin' back out. I'm gonna find me somebody myself.

LISA. Why don't you just do it with me? Just tonight.

CLINT (*pause. Looks at her*). Not tonight. Honey. Naw. Not you tonight. I got a taste for somethin' different.

LISA. I don't see why.

CLINT. I don't expect you to.

LISA. You could tell me.

CLINT. You wouldn't get it. (*Looks in the mirror.*) How do I look?

LISA. You look okay.

CLINT. Yeah, but do I look good?

LISA. You look good.

CLINT. How's my hair? (*He reaches up and pats it.*)

LISA. It's kinda messy.

CLINT. Come over here then. (*He pulls a comb out of his pocket and hands it toward her.*) Gimme a comb. (*He sits on the edge of the bed. She crawls up behind him and crouches on her knees. She begins combing his hair.)* Get a nice clean part.

LISA. I will.

CLINT. Not too far over.

LISA. I know. *(She finishes up. Hands him back the comb.)* Here.

CLINT *(pats his head again)*. Okay. What about my shoes? *(Without hesitation LISA crawls down onto the floor and begins retying his shoes. He reaches in his pocket and pulls out some money and puts it on the bed.)* Here. In case you want a Coke or somethin'.

LISA. Thanks.

CLINT. Don't be mad.

LISA. I ain't mad.

CLINT. Don't be.

LISA. I ain't. *(She finishes and sits back.)*

CLINT. I'll be back in a while. You go on an' wash your hair. Try not to look so scary.

LISA. Okay.

CLINT. See ya.

(He exits. Long pause. LISA gets up, walks over to the window and looks through the curtains. When she is certain he is gone she goes to the phone and dials.)

LISA. Hey. Is this the police? Yeah. I called a while back, about a missin' girl, about her bein' up at the state park. Remember? Well, I gotta talk fast, but I know where there's a girl and a boy that's missin'. They're, if you go down, go down by Huntsville, down south a Huntsville there's a road called Turkey Creek Road. Run down that road a ways and there's like a Golden Gallons, an' a tire place. And then there's some big electric plant. Go past that plant and there's a road that turns off to the left, just past Route 35, and goes up over some railroad tracks. Go back on that road a ways to where you see a creek, and past that, a little hollow place. And look there. That's where they are. Back in there. *(She hangs up. The phone rings immediately. She screams. Then she picks it up nervously, doesn't say anything for a second.)* Hello? *(Beat.)* No ma'am. No ma'am, the room hadn't been cleaned. Yeah. I'd 'preciate that. Bye. *(She hangs up and stares at the phone. Blackout.)*

SCENE 8

As lights come up, CLINT, LISA and ANGIE are seated on the ends of the bed, watching TV. They all seem uncomfortable.

ANGIE. Y'all don't have to watch this. If you want to watch somethin' else. I don't care.

LISA. This is okay. I'm sorry about how the room looks. They called down here and said they was gonna clean it, but nobody ever came.

ANGIE. I don't care.

CLINT. What do y'all wanna do?

ANGIE. I think I gotta go.

CLINT. You just got here.

ANGIE. I know. But I gotta go. It's late.

CLINT. It ain't late.

ANGIE. Yeah. It is.

CLINT. I thought you wanted to ride around some.

ANGIE. We already did. It got kinda boring.

CLINT. Well let's just watch some TV.

ANGIE *(sighs)*. Okay.

CLINT. Lisa could go get some beer.

LISA. I'll get carded.

CLINT. We can all go.

ANGIE. Nah. If you're gonna go I'd just as soon go home.

CLINT. I think you oughta stay. *(Pause.)* Maybe you'd have more fun if we fooled around some.

ANGIE. What?

CLINT. You know?

ANGIE. You me and her?

CLINT. Or just you and me. She can go out somewhere.

ANGIE. No way!

CLINT. What's wrong?

ANGIE. Nothin'. I just ain't foolin' around with you is all. *(She gets up.)*

CLINT. Where're you goin'?

ANGIE. Home.

CLINT *(rises)*. No ma'am.

ANGIE. What's your problem? *(She moves toward the door. He crosses to her quickly, grabbing her by the arm.)* Let go!

CLINT. No ma'am. I spent all day lookin' for you. Come on back here.

ANGIE. Let me go!

(She struggles. CLINT pushes her on the bed, on top of LISA.)

LISA. Ouch!

CLINT. Get out of the way! *(He shoves LISA on the floor.)*

LISA. Stop it! *(She gets up.)* She said she don't want to!

(CLINT backhands LISA across the face. She loses her balance and falls again. ANGIE has gotten up and is headed for the door. CLINT grabs her by the belt and pulls her back. She slaps him and he shoves her on the bed again. He gets on top of her and puts his hand over her mouth.)

CLINT. Calm down. *(LISA gets up slowly and looks at them. She moves toward the bathroom. CLINT ignores her.)* Just lemme git these jeans off. *(He reaches down to unzip ANGIE's jeans. She hits him hard on the nose.)* Fuck! *(He grabs at his nose and sits back. ANGIE pushes him and squirms out from under him. She rushes to the door.)* Stay there, you goddamn cunt!

(CLINT lunges at ANGIE. ANGIE gets the door open and standing there are two POLICEMEN. They all stare at one another for a moment.)

POLICEMAN #1. Ma'am?

ANGIE. What?

POLICEMAN #1. Are you Lisa Needham, ma'am?

ANGIE. Help me!

POLICEMAN #1. Are you Lisa Needham, ma'am?

ANGIE. No. I'm not. Help me.

POLICEMAN #2. Who are you, sir?

CLINT *(still holding his nose, talking through his hand)*. My name's Clint Needham.

POLICEMAN #2 *(to ANGIE)*. Is he any relation to you?

ANGIE. He was tryin' to kill me.

POLICEMAN #1. Is that true, sir?

CLINT. No. No. We was just...she was...we was just foolin' around. We ain't done nothin'.

POLICEMAN #1. What happened to your nose, sir?

CLINT. Nothin'. I got a cold.

ANGIE. I hit him. He was shovin' me on the bed. He was gonna kill me. *(Beat. The POLICEMEN stare at her.)* Help me!

POLICEMAN #1. Okay, ma'am. We'll help you. Sir? Could you just move slowly back into the room and turn to the wall? Could you just put your face to the wall and your hands behind your head, with your fingers interlocking?

CLINT *(starts to move)*. My nose is busted. Are you gonna do anything about my busted nose? *(He moves into the room as instructed.)*

POLICEMAN #2 *(seeing LISA in the back)*. Are you Miz Needham, ma'am?

LISA. Yeah. *(Beat.)* Is this somethin' about my babies?

POLICEMAN #1. No ma'am. This is something else. I wonder if you and Mr. Needham and this young lady would consent to come down to the police station with us?

CLINT. What for?

POLICEMAN #2. To answer some questions.

CLINT. 'Bout what?

POLICEMAN #2. About some murders.

CLINT *(turns back from the wall)*. No. We won't.

POLICEMAN #1. Then we'll have to place you and Miz Needham under arrest, sir.

CLINT. Under arrest?

POLICEMAN #1. Yessir.

CLINT *(turned to the police, with his hands still behind his head)*. Y'all are the goddamn end. You know that? Where'd you learn ta talk like that? Police school?

POLICEMAN #1 *(not understanding)*. I'm sorry, sir?

CLINT. That's it. You call me "sir" one more time an' I'm gonna have to rip your fuckin' face off. You unnerstand? *(He pulls his hands down. Neither of the POLICEMEN react, except to stare at him. Long pause.)*

POLICEMAN #1. Yes. Yes I do. *(Small beat.)* Sir. *(Lights fade out.)*

END ACT ONE

ACT TWO

SCENE 1

A police station interrogation room. There is a table and a couple of chairs. A tape recorder sits on the table. LISA sits in one of the chairs. She looks around nervously. She is clutching a red, plastic toy piano, about the size of a lunch box. One of the legs of the piano is broken. She stares off into space and then instantly is alert when a detective, BOB BURROWS, enters. He is a heavy-set man in a suit.

BURROWS *(pauses for a moment, looks at LISA)*. Miss Needham?

LISA. Mrs. Needham.

BURROWS. Mrs. Needham. My name is Bob Burrows. I'm a detective. For the police department. I'd like to ask you some questions

LISA. What for?

BURROWS. We think you might be able to help us. With some... really, very tragic, um, crimes. Help us with some crimes that have been committed in Alabama. How old are you, ma'am?

LISA. I just turned eighteen.

BURROWS. Good. Can you tell me, did anyone confer with you? About legal representation?

LISA. What?

BURROWS. By law, you are allowed to have an attorney present here for any questioning. Did anyone explain that to you?

LISA. Yeah.

BURROWS. And do you want an attorney?

LISA. Where's my husband?

BURROWS. Oh, I was unaware that your husband was an attorney.

LISA. He ain't. He's a car thief.

BURROWS. Oh.

LISA. I was just wonderin' where he was.

BURROWS. He's working with some other detectives.

LISA. On what?

BURROWS. Just some other questions. We have for him.

LISA. Oh.

BURROWS. Is there anything you want to tell me about your husband?

LISA. Are you crazy? *(Beat.)* I mean, no.

BURROWS. So, do you want a lawyer?

LISA. I don't need no lawyer.

BURROWS. Okey-dokey then, down to business. Mrs. Needham, I would like to show you some photographs and have you tell me whether or not you recognize any of these people. *(He pulls out three pictures and spreads them on the table in front of her. LISA stares for a moment. She rests her elbow on the table and cups her hand over her mouth. Pointing at each one.)* Now this young lady, do you recognize her?

LISA. No.

BURROWS. No?

LISA. No. I don't know any of them people.

BURROWS. What?

LISA (*taking her hand from her mouth*). I said, "I don't know any of them people."

BURROWS. Well, that's interesting.

LISA (*puts her elbow back up and covers her mouth*). How come?

BURROWS. What about this one here, this man. Are you sure you never saw him before?

LISA. Yeah.

BURROWS. That's funny, 'cause he remembers you.

LISA. I don't know him.

BURROWS. Is there something in your hand?

LISA. What?

BURROWS. Are you licking something in your hand?

LISA (*sits up, puts her hands to her side, irritated*). No.

BURROWS (*very satisfied*). Well, all right then. I wonder, would you just sit back, just sit there and listen to this. (*He takes out a tape and puts it in the tape recorder and presses play. A tape of LISA's first phone call to the police is heard.*)

LISA (*on tape*). "Hello? This the police station?... Um, no. I don't guess it's an emergency. I just got some information—"

BURROWS (*turns the sound down*). Do you recognize that?

LISA (*looks at the floor*). Yes.

BURROWS. And what do you have to say?

LISA (*looking up with a small smile*). Did you record that other one I made too? About them other people?

BURROWS (*shocked*). Then you don't deny making the calls?

LISA. No.

BURROWS. Then... do you want to make a statement?

LISA. What do you want to know?

BURROWS. I want to know the truth.

LISA *(getting to business and pointing at a picture).* Okay. This first girl, she was a girl we picked up outside the Quick Stop in Fayette. She was runnin' away from the home, and she ...

BURROWS. Wait! Stop. Let me, let me get somebody else in here, and a recorder, I mean, a court reporter, and, and a blank tape. Okay. Wait.

LISA. Okay. *(Blackout.)*

SCENE 2

Same as before except that a TRANSCRIBER and an-other detective, HUGH, have joined the scene. LISA is in mid-statement.

LISA. She was awful young, I thought, but Clint, he was happy ta have her, ya know. He was doin' stuff to her an—

BURROWS. What kind of "stuff"?

LISA. Well, like he was, you know, doin' it to her. He had her handcuffed ta the bed, and he put her on that bed, and he kinda put her at an angle before he did it to her. I think he busted somethin' in her.

BURROWS. So he raped her.

LISA. Yeah.

BURROWS. You don't care?

LISA. It wadn't nothin' new. *(Trying to explain.)* He did shit like that all the time.

BURROWS *(pauses. Stares at her).* Go on.

LISA. Well, the next day, he tole me I hadda kill her. He tole me how I needed ta do it and where ta take her. He give me his gun. *(Beat.)* Well, I hadda go git my babies, 'cuz of how I was missin' 'em somethin' awful. So me and the girl, we went up ta Clint's mama's an' got my babies.

BURROWS. You have children?

LISA. Twins.

BURROWS. Where are they now?

LISA. Back up at Clint's mama's. They stay up there mostly. Clint, he don't, well, he don't like 'em much.

BURROWS. These are infants?

LISA. Naw. They're two and a half.

BURROWS. Two? And a half? *(Beat. She doesn't answer.)* Go on.

LISA. Anyway, me and her went up, and I got my babies, and then—

BURROWS. Under what pretense did you have her in the car?

LISA. I tole her I was takin' her home. She wanted to go home. So I took her up to that park, up where Clint tole me to—

BURROWS. Where was Clint?

LISA. Off.

BURROWS. Off?

LISA. Off somewhere. He was ta meet me. Later at his mama's. So I took the girl up to the park, up where Clint said to. And then I took out the gun. I took her over to a tree and I made her sit down under it. Clint, he tole me to shoot her in the chest. But I thought, maybe I could do it somehow so that she would just fall asleep and it wouldn't hurt her none. So, I had me some needles, some hypodermic needles I got a while back, from this girl in the group home. And I had some Liquid Drano. So I pulled the Drano up inta the needle and I made her sit there and I put it in her neck.

BURROWS. You injected Drano into her neck?

LISA. In her neck, and then in her arms, 'cause it didn't seem to be puttin' her to sleep. She just kept tellin' me it was burnin' her. It was burnin'. But it wadn't doin' nothin', I don't think. For a long time I watched her but she wadn't dyin'. So then I figured Clint was right. I made her stand up and walk over ta that cliff. Then I just said, "Turn around, look over there, look at them pretty trees," an' I shot her in the back of the head. She just fell then, just fell off the cliff. I couldn't even see her body where she fell. She didn't cry or nothin'. (*Long pause.*)

BURROWS. And, where were your babies, while you were shooting this girl?

LISA. In the back seat. Asleep.

BURROWS. And, um, Mrs. Needham, refresh my memory. Why did you kill her?

LISA. Clint tole me to.

BURROWS. You do everything he tells you to do.

LISA. Yeah.

BURROWS. Why?

LISA. 'Cause.

BURROWS. Because you love him?

LISA. No sir.

BURROWS. Why then?

LISA. You don't want to know.

BURROWS. Oh, yes I do.

LISA. He'd a killed me. If I hadn't done it.

BURROWS. But you said he was "off" somewhere.

LISA. Yeah.

BURROWS. Then why didn't you just let the girl go?

LISA *(this idea is new to her)*. I dunno. It's just that...he would of known.

BURROWS. How?

LISA. I'm a bad liar.

BURROWS. Christ. *(Long pause.)*

HUGH. Why'd ya call us, Miz Needham?

LISA *(thinks)*. I hated...I hated ta think a her down there. Maybe gettin' eaten up by birds or somethin'. *(Long pause.)* She looked like Joanie Cunningham.

HUGH. Really.

BURROWS. Who?

HUGH. Joanie Cunningham. From *Happy Days*.

BURROWS. Oh. I never watched that program.

LISA. She looked just like her. *(Long pause.)*

BURROWS. Well then. That would seem to cover Kelly. What can you tell us about Steve Culverhouse?

LISA. Who?

BURROWS. The young man you shot.

LISA. Oh yeah. Him. Well, I picked him and his girlfriend up one night, off the side of the road. But I guess he ain't dead?

BURROWS. No, Lisa. You left him for dead, of course, but he managed to make it back to the road and flag down a trucker.

LISA. His girlfriend was a retard.

BURROWS. What?

LISA. She was. She was a retard. But that didn't mean she wadn't nice. I guess Clint liked her okay. But then, he said I hadda kill her too.

BURROWS. He raped Carol Brown?

LISA. Nah. She wanted to do it. She was a retard.

BURROWS. I don't think she was retarded.

LISA. Oh yeah she was. That guy, he said as how he came home one night and she was playin' pin-the-tail-on-the-donkey all by herself.

BURROWS *(confused)*. Go back please.

LISA. That guy, her boyfriend, he tole me that. In the car.

BURROWS. Can you start from the beginning. From the first time you saw Steve Culverhouse and Carol Brown.

LISA. Okay.

TRANSCRIBER. Excuse me.

BURROWS. Yes?

TRANSCRIBER. Is pin-the-tail-on-the-donkey hyphenated?

HUGH. Yeah. I b'lieve it is.

TRANSCRIBER. Thank you. *(Blackout.)*

SCENE 3

Same room. STEVE CULVERHOUSE sits alone, smoking a cigarette. He turns the matchbook over and over in his hands. Finally, a large, well-dressed man enters. He is CARL SHEFFIELD, Lisa's attorney. Throughout the questioning he consults notes and takes notes.

CARL *(offering his hand)*. Mr. Culverhouse.

STEVE *(stands. Shakes his hand)*. Yessir.

CARL. I'm Carl Sheffield.

STEVE. Yessir. I know.

CARL. Thank you for coming down today.

STEVE. I thought I had to.

CARL. I just want to ask you some questions. You understand, I'm not a policeman.

STEVE. Yessir. You're that girl's lawyer.

CARL. That's right. I'm appointed, by the court, to defend her.

STEVE. Yessir.

CARL. Now, I need to hear some things from you. But you are not required to tell me anything that would incriminate you.

STEVE. Nothin' would.

CARL *(smiles)*. Of course not. That's just something we say. *(Beat.)* Now then. What I would like, is if you could tell me everything you remember about that night. The twelfth. I know this is difficult for you, but why don't you start by telling me what you and your girlfriend Carol were doing that night.

STEVE. We was out walkin'.

CARL. To where?

STEVE. Nowhere. We was just out. *(Sighs.)* It's like I said before. I feel bad about this. But I couldn't offer Carol a lot in the way of fun. Ya know? 'Cause, we was flat busted. An' I had been at work all day and she was home. She had been in that trailer all day an' I knew she wanted ta go out an' do somethin', only I didn't have the money. So, I said, well, let's go for a walk.

CARL. It was a nice evening?

STEVE. Yeah. We liked to walk on the road and look for nuts and bolts. Washers an' stuff. You'd be surprised how many you find. They're usually pretty rusty an' stuff, but you can clean 'em up. They're just as good as new if you clean 'em up. *(Long pause.)* Is that what you want to hear? Really?

CARL. Yes.

STEVE. Well, okay. We was out walkin'. Then that girl pulled up, and she asked did we want to go for a ride. She said she had just moved here, and she was lonely. She didn't know anybody. So we said okay.

CARL. Can you describe Mrs. Needham's appearance to me, when you first saw her.

STEVE. She looked okay.

CARL. Did she seem clean? Um, neat and trim?

STEVE. Her hair was kinda dirty.

CARL. Were there any visible bruises, or scars?

STEVE. Not that I seen.

CARL. Maybe signs of a black eye?

STEVE. Nah. She had circles under her eyes, maybe. Like she hadn't been sleepin'. But she seemed okay. *(Beat.)*

CARL. How long had you and Carol been living together?

STEVE. About eight or nine months.

CARL *(looking at his notes)*. And I'm assuming she didn't work because she was retarded?

STEVE. She wadn't retarded.

CARL. Oh. Um, maybe I'm confused, but in the police report she's listed as retarded.

STEVE. No way!

CARL. Perhaps they're mistaken.

STEVE. She wadn't retarded. *(Beat.)* She was sweet. An' a little slow maybe. But she wadn't retarded.

CARL *(trying to explain the mistake)*. Then, when you told Mrs. Needham that she played pin-the-tail-on-the-donkey by herself, you weren't intending to imply that she was retarded.

STEVE *(looks extremely uncomfortable)*. No.

CARL. You were just making conversation.

STEVE. I don't know. *(Beat.)* It wadn't nothin'. I was just ... Carol was in the back seat.

CARL *(nods)*. All right then. That's fine. *(Looks at his notes.)* So you and Carol had been living together for eight or nine months.

STEVE. Yeah.

CARL. And you're currently employed at a machine shop?

STEVE. It's a Snapper dealership.

CARL. Snapper?

STEVE. Lawn mowers. I fix lawn mowers.

CARL. Is that interesting work?

STEVE. No.

CARL. So Mrs. Needham pulled up and she asked if you wanted to go for a ride.

STEVE. Yeah.

CARL. Would you ride around often, with other people, or friends?

STEVE. No sir.

CARL. But Carol would.

STEVE. I don't follow.

CARL *(looking at his notes again)*. According to Mrs. Needham, Carol told her that she would ride around, or get rides home a lot.

STEVE. Carol told her that? When'd she tell her that?

CARL. It's something that came up in Mrs. Needham's statement.

STEVE. What'd she say exactly?

CARL. Mrs. Needham related that Carol did not object to having, you know, relations with Mr. Needham. That Carol would sometimes use sex as a way to get rides home.

STEVE. Why would she say that?

CARL. It was...she just said that Carol said that she had
never done it—I mean, had sexual intercourse with you,
but that she had previously had numerous partners. I'm
not sure in what context—

STEVE. That man raped Carol.

CARL. Technically, of course—

STEVE. Don't mock me!

CARL. Believe me, I'm not—

STEVE *(with a lot of effort)*. That man raped Carol. And
then they took...they took Carol in the woods. They shot
her in the back of the head. They shot her and left her
there and I saw her body. They left her in a stream, mister. She was purple. Okay? She was purple. And maybe
she was retarded. And what? Does that make it okay?

CARL. I never meant to imply—

STEVE. Her skin was cracked open. Her skin was cracked
open and she was leakin' water through her skin. *(Long
pause.)*

CARL. I just have a few more questions Mr. Culverhouse.
(Beat. He forges ahead.) While you were in the car with
Mrs. Needham, did you make contact with Mr. Need-
ham?

STEVE. Yes.

CARL. How?

STEVE. He came up behind us in his car and started
talkin' to her on the CB.

CARL. What did he say?

STEVE. He said, "Hey up there. Hey. Y'all lookin' for
somethin' to do?"

CARL. How did he address Mrs. Needham.

STEVE. He pretended like he didn't know her.

CARL. What did he say next?

STEVE. He said, "Hey. Why don't we go down ta Atlanta? Why don't we all go out and drink. Hey." Stuff like that.

CARL. And what happened.

STEVE. Carol wanted to go. So we said okay. Then, then that girl, she told him okay over the radio.

CARL. Did Mrs. Needham seem agitated at all?

STEVE. How?

CARL. Frightened or nervous?

STEVE. No. She didn't seem like nothin' was wrong.

CARL. What happened next?

STEVE. That guy said, "Pull over here. Down that road. Then we can make some plans." So she pulled down this dirt road a ways. Not too far. And he pulled in behind us.

CARL. He was right behind you. Directly behind you?

STEVE. Yeah. He pulled up behind us not long after we got in her car. He pulled in behind us and got out of his car and walked up to my side of the car. I said "Hey" and he said "Hey" and we talked about maybe where we wanted to go. Then, well, I had to take a whiz, so I excused myself and got out and went in the woods a little bit.

CARL. Had you been drinking?

STEVE. No sir, I'm a Christian.

CARL. I'm sorry, I didn't know. So you went off in the woods to relieve yourself.

STEVE. Yeah, and then I come back out and she's standin' in the road waitin' for me with a gun.

CARL. Did Mr. Needham have a gun as well?

STEVE. None I saw.

CARL. But Mrs. Needham did.

STEVE. She had a big fuckin' gun.

CARL. All right.

STEVE. And she told me to start walkin' down the road. I looked back and that man was down by his car with Carol. He was puttin' Carol in his car.

CARL. What do you mean by "putting her in the car." Was he shoving her, or pushing her?

STEVE. No. They was just walkin'. *(Beat.)* You're tryin' to say it again! You're tryin' to say that she wanted to go off with him.

CARL. No I'm not.

STEVE. Fuck you.

CARL. I—

STEVE. I mean it! Fuck you. *(Long pause.)*

CARL. All right then. What happened next.

STEVE. I said, "What are you doin'? What are you doin' with my girlfriend?" and she told me to shut up and walk down into this clearing a ways back. Then she said to stop. And then she shot me in the back. *(Beat.)* I fell on my face.

CARL. And was there anything in Mrs. Needham's behavior, anything to make you think that what she was doing, she was doing because she was being coerced? That what she was doing, she was doing against her will?

STEVE. No.

CARL. Well, was there anything in Mr. Needham's tone or manner that seemed threatening? That seemed to imply, "I'm in charge here. I'm in control."

STEVE. Mister, if it was anything, it was just the opposite. She was into it. She was doin' just what she wanted.

CARL. What makes you say that?

STEVE. You could tell. She was wearin' a big smile.

CARL. But you said your back was to her.

STEVE *(calmly)*. I looked back. One time. She was smilin'. After that I could feel it.

CARL. And after—

STEVE. I don't have anything else to say.

CARL. But—

STEVE *(stands)*. This interview is over, mister.

CARL *(considers)*. Well, then, I thank you for your time and your cooperation, Mr. Culverhouse. I will be asking you more questions in court, you know.

STEVE. And I'll tell the judge what I'm tellin' you now. I hope they give her the chair.

CARL. We'll see about that.

STEVE. How long you lived in Alabama?

CARL. All my life.

STEVE. Then you know what I do. They'll give her the chair. *(CARL starts to leave. STEVE stops him.)* Look, mister? I just want you to know, the thing was, I never even asked her to sleep with me. I never asked her 'cause I loved her.

CARL. I'm sorry.

STEVE. Then give her the chair.

CARL. She's my client.

STEVE. Give her the chair.

CARL. I wouldn't be much of a lawyer.

STEVE. Give her the chair. *(They stare at one another. Slow fadeout.)*

SCENE 4

Same room. LISA sits, fidgeting with her hair. CARL is pacing.

CARL. You've got to help me out here, Lisa.

LISA. I already told 'em I did it.

CARL. I know. But maybe you didn't understand, that you didn't have to tell the police anything. That you probably really needed a lawyer.

LISA. I told 'em I didn't want a lawyer.

CARL. I know. There's not a lot we can do about that. But we do have something we can work with.

LISA. I don't mind bein' in jail.

CARL. Lisa, we're not talking about jail. I don't think you understand. The state is going to ask for the death penalty. They want to give you the electric chair. They don't care how old you are.

LISA. Oh.

CARL. Right, "Oh." "Oh" is right. *(Pause.)*

LISA. But I already told 'em I did it.

CARL. I know. But the thing we can work on is why you did it.

LISA. I told 'em that too.

CARL. Yes, Lisa. Just...just listen for a minute. Okay?

LISA. Are you mad at me?

CARL. No.

LISA. Them other people askin' questions was real mad at me.

CARL. Well, you killed some people, Lisa. That doesn't really make you popular.

LISA. I guess you're right.

CARL. They think you killed those girls out of mean-spirit-
edness. Out of being mean. But I don't think that's why
you did it.

LISA. You don't?

CARL. No.

LISA *(looks at him)*. You ain't gonna yell at me?

CARL. I rarely yell. Let's just work this out together. Now,
total honesty here, why did you kill them?

LISA. I had to.

CARL. Because of Clint?

LISA. Clint said I had to.

CARL. You were afraid of him.

LISA *(quietly)*. Yeah.

CARL. Did he hit you?

LISA *(long pause)*. Sometimes.

CARL. He's a big guy.

LISA. He's mean.

CARL. And you were scared of him. *(LISA nods.)* But
there are some difficult questions.

LISA. Like what?

CARL. Like why, when Clint was miles away, you still had
to kill the girl. Why didn't you let her go?

LISA. I said already.

CARL. You said you're a bad liar.

LISA. I suck.

CARL. Then why didn't you just leave him? You could
have driven anywhere.

LISA *(shakes her head)*. I couldn't.

CARL. Why not?

LISA. I don't know.

CARL. That's not good enough.

LISA. Well I don't know.

CARL *(exasperated)*. Lisa!

LISA. Look—Clint found me. He found me at my mama's. He found me when they took me off ta the group home. He found me when I was in the hospital, and didn't nobody tell him where I was. He just found me. He knows how.

CARL. The Department of Social Services told him where you were. You're his wife. *(Long pause.)*

LISA. That's not what he said.

CARL. So you never thought to yourself, just to let the girl go?

LISA. No. Sorry.

CARL. And the same thing, with Steve Culverhouse?

LISA. Clint was right behind me. He woulda seen.

CARL. He says he had already driven off with the girl. That he didn't know what you were doing.

LISA. He did?

CARL. Yes.

LISA. That ain't so.

CARL. Lisa, the woman that was in your hotel when the police came didn't press charges. She was on her way to Florida. Didn't want to be bothered. He'll probably plead guilty to lesser charges in exchange for his testimony and be out in a couple of years.

LISA. I don't get it.

CARL. He didn't pull the trigger. *(Long pause.)*

LISA. Well. He was there when I shot that guy, but I guess I don't got no way to prove it.

CARL. And Carol? He wasn't anywhere near you and Carol.

LISA. No. Me and Carol was alone.

CARL *(slowly)*. Then why?

LISA *(quietly)*. You don't understand.

CARL. No, Lisa. I think I do understand. But I'm not on the jury. And those are the people we have to make understand. You see?

LISA. I guess.

CARL. Lisa, whether or not they believe your story is going to depend on whether or not they believe you. And you are not a convincing witness. *(LISA laughs.)* See? Like that Lisa. Like that. Why is that funny?

LISA *(shrugs, grinning)*. I dunno.

CARL. You smile at all the wrong times.

LISA *(puts her hand over her mouth)*. Sorry.

CARL *(reaches over gently and lowers her hand)*. Are you sorry you killed those girls?

LISA. Yes.

CARL. Really?

LISA. I guess.

CARL. Lisa!

LISA. They was gonna die anyway.

CARL. I don't know what you mean.

LISA. There's just people as are gonna die. Just people as are gonna get killed. It's the way it is.

CARL. Fate?

LISA *(trying to explain)*. No. They got in the car with me.

CARL. That's why you killed them?

LISA. No. That's why they died. *(Beat. She tries a new tact.)* Now you, would you of ever got in the car with me?

CARL. No.

LISA. See? They did. Because they're of that type. It's just a thing that happens to a type. And it woulda kept happenin' forever. *(Long pause.)*

CARL. That's why you called the police.

LISA. No.

CARL. Yes, Lisa. Yes it is.

LISA. I don't know why I called the police.

CARL. Don't tell the jury that. Tell the jury that you called to stop it. You were frightened to death and you would rather be in jail than out there again with Clint.

LISA. But I wadn't thinkin' that.

CARL. I don't care. You say it.

LISA. It won't work.

CARL. It won't work if you don't make it work.

LISA. You tell 'em what you want but they ain't gonna believe it. They'll know just by lookin' at me. They'll know that it never even occurred to me that I didn't hafta do it.

CARL. It really didn't?

LISA. No. *(Pause.)*

CARL. Where's your little piano?

LISA. Who told you that?

CARL. Detective Burrows. He said you held on to it like crazy.

LISA. So.

CARL. He said your daddy gave it to you.

LISA. So.

CARL. That it was all you took with you when you left home. At fifteen.

LISA. I took all my clothes.

CARL. That's not the point.

LISA *(shakes her head)*. Go on then, say what you want.

CARL. It's not just me, though, Lisa. It's what you say too.

LISA. I ain't gonna say that crap.

CARL. Do you want to die? Is that it?

LISA. It doesn't matter.

CARL. It does!

LISA. It doesn't! You tell me one way that it matters.

CARL. It matters a lot.

LISA. No it don't. That girl I killed, and them two other people, if I hadn't called the police, if that guy hadn't of lived, wouldn't anybody even know they was gone.

CARL. I'm sure somebody—

LISA. No you ain't. You ain't sure. *(Beat.)*

CARL. Well, I suppose it's possible...

LISA. It's more than "possible." It's the goddamn truth. *(Pause.)*

CARL. Now that's precisely the sort of thing you should not say in the courtroom. *(LISA stares at him. Lights fade out.)*

SCENE 5

A trailer on the grounds of the prison. It looks amazingly like the old motel rooms they used to live in, except even more bare. There are no chairs. There is one bed, relatively neatly made up with an old bedspread and pillows. The door opens and CLINT enters. He is cleaned up a bit, wearing a clean T-shirt and jeans. A voice from off says "Wait there."

CLINT. Okay.

(He looks around for a place to sit, sees only the bed, and sits down carefully, perched on the edge. Almost right away, LISA enters, wearing jeans, a work shirt, and flip flops. The GUARD sticks his head in.)

GUARD. Okay. You two got thirty minutes. At twenty-five minutes, I give a warnin' knock on the door. Then at thirty, I open it. There are no surveillance cameras in the trailer. Got it?

CLINT. Yessir. Thank you.

GUARD. You got a watch?

CLINT. Yessir.

GUARD. Watch the time then. You don't want no surprises. *(He closes the door.)*

CLINT. Yessir. *(He looks at his watch.)* Okay.

LISA. Hey.

CLINT. Oh, hey, honey! *(Laughs.)* C'mere and gimme a hug. *(She goes to him. They hug awkwardly.)* Here, sit down. *(He pats the bed.)*

LISA. I don't mind standin'.

CLINT. Okay, okay. Hey. You look great.

LISA. Thanks.

CLINT. I like them sandals.

LISA. Thanks. *(Pause.)*

CLINT. This is kinda weird, ain't it?

LISA. Yeah.

CLINT. You sure you don't wanna sit down? Just ta get off your feet? I mean, there ain't no chairs.

LISA. Okay then. *(She sits on the bed. He sits down beside her.)* How are you then?

CLINT. Oh, hell, honey, I'm fine. When hadn't I been fine?

LISA. Never I guess. *(Pause.)*

CLINT. Look, honey, we don't, we don't gotta do nothin' here. I'm just so happy to see you and talk to you and be able to touch you even. Would it be okay if we just sat here and I held your hand?

LISA. I guess so. *(She doesn't offer her hand. CLINT takes it.)*

CLINT. Lisa honey, I gotta start out by sayin' one thing.

LISA. What's that?

CLINT. I am so sorry.

LISA. It ain't your fault.

CLINT. It is too my fault! Shit, honey, wouldn't none of this mess happened if it wadn't for me.

LISA. You didn't kill nobody.

CLINT. In a way I did.

LISA. How?

CLINT. I give you the gun, didn't I? And in a way, I guess I give you the motivation.

LISA. You mean, motivation, like sayin', "Go kill that girl." You mean like that?

CLINT *(pauses)*. Now, Lisa. I unnerstand, how you had to say things in court. Ugly things like that. I unnerstand all them lawyers, they had you sayin' things just so you could not look so bad. But, honey, this is you and me sittin' here. Clint and Lisa and nobody else. Now you can say the truth ta me. *(Pause.)* You didn't really mean all that stuff, did ya?

LISA. How do you know what I said in there?

CLINT. I read it in the paper, honey. Every mornin' they'd bring me the paper and say, "Hey Clint! Look what your wife's sayin' today. Your wife's sayin' you're the bad-dest thing since King Kong, man."

LISA. They brung you a paper to your cell?

CLINT. Yeah.

LISA. In here we only got one room we can read the paper in. I only get to go down there one time a week.

CLINT. That's too bad.

LISA. And here, we don't get outa jail after eighteen months. Are you glad ta be outa jail?

CLINT. Well, yeah, I'm glad. Only, I'm sorry I was ever in it 'cause it meant I couldn't come and help you. I couldn't be there for you.

LISA. That's okay.

CLINT. No it ain't, honey! Jesus. Girl, listen ta me. This is the worse thing that ever happened to you and now you got ta sit in here and face it all by yourself and I feel terrible about that. I feel terrible. I just want to love you and make you feel better. That's all.

LISA *(quietly)*. Okay then. I feel better.

CLINT. You do?

LISA. Yeah I do.

CLINT. An' you didn't mean none of that stuff you said about me. Tell me that.

LISA. I didn't mean it.

CLINT. Okay then. You did what was right, honey. Don't feel bad. You were just tryin' ta protect yourself, 'cause wadn't nobody there to do it for you.

LISA. That's right.

CLINT. Okay. *(Beat.)* That's settled then. *(Pause.)* So what else is new?

LISA. Nothin' really.

CLINT. What about the appeal? Your lawyer's got a appeal goin', right?

LISA. I guess so. Yeah.

CLINT. How's it goin'?

LISA. Okay, I guess.

CLINT. Good, good. *(Hugs her suddenly.)* Aw, honey! It's so good ta see you.

LISA *(into his chest)*. It's good ta see you too, Clint. *(Starts to reach down to her pocket.)* I wanna give you somethin'.

CLINT *(delighted)*. Oh yeah?

LISA. Yeah.

CLINT. What is it?

LISA *(digs in her pocket. Pulls out a dollar)*. Here.

CLINT. A dollar?

LISA. It's all the money I got but you can take it.

CLINT. What do I need a dollar for, honey?

LISA. I just wanted to give you somethin'. I gotta go now. *(She stands up quickly, crosses to the door.)*

CLINT. What? *(He follows her.)*

LISA *(starts knocking on the door)*. I gotta go. *(Shouts.)* Hey! Hey!

CLINT *(takes her arm)*. It ain't time yet. *(Looks at his watch, thinks.)* It ain't even half time yet.

LISA *(shouting)*. Open the door!

CLINT. Why don't you wanna stay?

LISA. I got a lot to do. *(Shouts and pounds with her free hand.)* Open the goddamn door! *(The door opens suddenly.)*

GUARD. What is it?

LISA. I wanna go now.

GUARD. Your time's not up.

LISA. I wanna go back to my cell now please.

GUARD. Is there a problem?

LISA. No, he's just faster than most. *(She steps out past him.)*

GUARD *(only slightly puzzled)*. Okay then. *(Turns his back to CLINT, blocking the door. Yells.)* Walt? *(Beat.)* Come get Mrs. Needham. She wants to go back. *(Turns back to*

CLINT.) Okay, Mr. Needham. I'll escort you back as soon as your wife's cleared the yard.

CLINT. Can't I just talk to her?

GUARD. No sir.

CLINT *(yells over the GUARD's shoulder).* Lisa? What'd I do?

LISA *(off. Yells back, retreating).* Bye, Clint!

CLINT *(yells again).* How come you're mad? *(Beat. No answer.)* Lisa! They took the babies! They put 'em in a foster home! *(No answer.)* Goddamn it!

GUARD. Sometimes they turn in here. I seen it happen more than once. They lose their taste for men.

CLINT *(stares at him a moment).* Fuck you.

GUARD *(shrugs).* Sometimes it happens is all. It's natural.

CLINT. She ain't never loved nobody but me, mister. Nobody but me.

GUARD. I'm just sayin'.

CLINT. You don't know shit. *(They stand. Blackout.)*

SCENE 6

Prison visiting room. CARL is waiting, reading over some papers. He seems tired. The GUARD enters, followed by LISA, carrying her toy piano.

GUARD. Here she is.

CARL. Thanks. *(GUARD exits.)* Lisa.

LISA. Hey.

CARL. I see you have your piano.

LISA. Yeah.

CARL. Shall we? *(He gestures toward the chair.)*

LISA. Okay. *(She sits.)*

CARL. I filed for the appeal. I don't have any real sense of what will happen, though, to be honest. The review usually takes quite a while. *(Beat.)* I say "usually" but I don't really know. I've never represented anybody on death row. But, I think at any rate, that your time is best spent now, in going back over the details, back over your testimony, and getting it right. In the event that we're granted another trial.

LISA. I'm sorry I made you so mad.

CARL. You didn't make me mad.

LISA. I know I didn't do good.

CARL. I don't know why you say that.

LISA. 'Cause I lost.

CARL. Well, I'm sorry not to have won for you. I think that some of my tactics may have ... alienated the jury.

LISA *(laughs)*. You pissed 'em off.

CARL. Yes. Well.

LISA. Half of them guys beat the shit outa their wives. And them wives, they say, "Shit, I git beat up, I don't go killin' nobody over it."

CARL. You could be right.

LISA. It's okay. I wish you wouldn't feel bad.

CARL. For Christ's sake, Lisa! You're going to the electric chair.

LISA. I still wish you wouldn't feel bad. It ain't your fault.

CARL. I just ... let me feel bad, if I want to feel bad. *(Pause.)* Are you getting everything you need here?

LISA. I guess. I did like it better before I lost. I don't get to see nobody else now. I gotta eat by myself.

CARL. You liked being around other prisoners?

LISA. They wadn't all bad.

CARL. Well, I'm sorry you had so much time to get to know them.

LISA. But this ain't so bad. I got my own room. And they let me go outside every day.

CARL. That's good. (*Hands her an envelope.*) These are the transcripts of your testimony. I want you to start by reading back over what you said, and seeing if there's anything you left out, that you can remember now.

LISA. How long before they kill me?

CARL. What?

LISA. How long?

CARL. But what about the appeal?

LISA. Yeah, but after that.

CARL. I'm hoping to reverse the judge's decision.

LISA. Okay, but after that.

CARL (*sighs*). Well, there's only one other prisoner here on death row, and it's been ten years since she was convicted.

LISA (*quietly pleased*). Wow.

CARL (*shaking his head*). I can't even begin to understand you.

LISA. Yeah. But I appreciate that you try.

(*Long pause. CARL stares at her. He looks as if he might cry. He looks down at his notes. Beat.*)

CARL (*quietly*). Do you mind if we talk about this later? I'm more tired than I thought.

LISA. Okay. (*He starts to get his things together. She pushes the piano toward him.*) Here.

CARL. What?

LISA. It's all I got, an' I want to give it to you.

CARL. I can't take this.

LISA. Yes you can. *(She pushes it in front of him.)* I wish it wadn't busted.

CARL. This is too precious to you. I can't.

LISA. But all the keys still work. See? *(She plinks a couple of keys. CARL studies her.)* Go on. Take it. *(Pause. He stares at it.)* Look, I want to give it to you. *(Small beat. Conceding something, to get him to take it.)* It's like you said. It's important to me. *(CARL looks at her, then at the piano, then slowly, he taps out the opening to "Mary Had a Little Lamb" on it.)* Hey! That's good! I couldn't never play nothin' on it.

CARL. Anybody can play that.

LISA. Not me.

CARL. Really?

LISA. Daddy just give it to me. He didn't show me how it worked.

CARL. That's a shame. *(Standing.)* It is. Come around here. *(She hesitates.)* Come on. I'll show you.

LISA. Okay I guess. *(She gets up, comes around the table.)*

CARL. Okay. Now, sit down. *(She sits.)* Now this, is not a full keyboard, obviously. But here, you have your white keys, and your black keys. Each key is a note, and each note has a name. Here. See this? This is the key to know. This is the middle C.

LISA *(tapping it)*. Middle C.

CARL *(tapping)*. Up two to E.

LISA *(tapping slowly)*. C, D, E.

CARL. Good. Now watch. *(Taps out the first notes of the song, just up to the point where it skips to G, and stops.)* Try that far.

LISA (*to herself, picking out the tune and naming the notes. CARL helps her out along the way*). E D C D, E E E, DDD, E. (*Looks up, smiling.*) Hey!

CARL (*points*). Now G twice. (*LISA reaches out, taps G twice.*) Okay. Now, back to the beginning. E, D, C, D, E E E... (*LISA plays it.*) One more E. (*She plays it. CARL reaches over her shoulder, finishes the song, playing and singing.*) "Whose fleece was white as snow."

LISA (*mimics him, playing and singing*). "Whose fleece was white as snow."

CARL. Right back to middle C.

LISA (*taps the middle C again, looks at the piano, looks up*). Teach me another one.

CARL. Okay. (*Pulling a chair up next to hers.*) Move over. (*He takes the piano.*) Now pay attention. (*He starts to play "Jingle Bells." LISA watches. Slow fadeout.*)

END OF PLAY

DIRECTOR'S NOTES

DIRECTOR'S NOTES